IN MY HEAD

A Young Person's Guide To Understanding Mental Health

LOUISE BATY

IN MY HEAD

Peer reviewed by Mayvrill Freeston-Roberts, BACP Accredited and Registered Counsellor and Psychotherapist

An Hachette UK Company
www.hachette.co.uk

Vie Books, an imprint of Summersdale Publishers Ltd
Part of Octopus Publishing Group Limited
Carmelite House
50 Victoria Embankment
LONDON
EC4Y 0DZ
UK

www.summersdale.com

Printed and bound in Poland

ISBN: 978-1-80007-195-7

Substantial discounts on bulk quantities of Summersdale books are available to corporations, professional associations and other organizations. For details contact general enquiries: telephone: +44 (0) 1243 771107 or email: enquiries@summersdale.com.

To J & J, who have always been excellent listeners, advice givers and cheerleaders during even the trickiest of times. Thank you for everything.

CONTENTS

INTRODUCTION

Hello! Welcome to *In My Head*. Chances are, you've picked up this book or someone else has given it to you as a helpful gift, because there's a lot going on for you right now.

From the age of 11 onwards, life starts to shift in a big way. Physical changes, mood swings, overpowering emotions... sound familiar?

It may feel as though you're the only one going through all this but you're not alone, honest! Every young person experiences a variety of challenges as they navigate the somewhat bumpy path through the pre-teen and teenage years, and beyond.

This book explains why you may feel like you do and includes easy-to-follow explanations about physical and mental changes and also neurodiversity – which simply means that not everyone's brain works in exactly the same way.

There are tips for coping with tricky issues such as one-sided or unhealthy friendships and problems at school, along with advice on putting together your own personalized self-care toolkit.

You'll find handy fill-in pages for tracking your moods, lifestyle habits and low mood triggers along with straight-forward information about common mental health issues.

Sadly, with one in seven teenagers experiencing mental health issues worldwide it's wise to be prepared for tricky times that may arise so that you can move forward to happier times. This book aims to give you the knowledge and the power to do just that.

CHAPTER ONE:

IS IT ALL IN MY HEAD?

This chapter will explain what's going on inside that head of yours, covering simple science, hormones, mental health and neurodiversity – because in order to understand your emotions and mood changes, it's helpful to first understand what may be causing them.

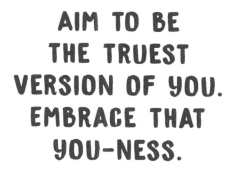

AIM TO BE
THE TRUEST
VERSION OF YOU.
EMBRACE THAT
YOU-NESS.

MATT HAIG

INSIDE YOUR BRAIN

Ever wondered what's going on in there, in your head?

Well, first things first, let's get this out in the open. You are a living, breathing miracle.

Yes, you!

Every single day as you sit in class or catch the bus or chat to your friends or watch TV, truly AMAZING things are happening inside that brain of yours.

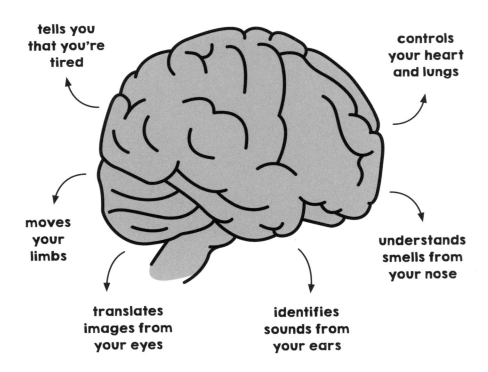

tells you that you're tired

controls your heart and lungs

moves your limbs

understands smells from your nose

translates images from your eyes

identifies sounds from your ears

It's mind-boggling really, which is *entirely* appropriate for the situation.

Think of your brain as your body's control centre or HQ. Take a look at the diagram opposite to see a few things it does without you even noticing.

Your brain doesn't just tell you things, like when you need sleep or a sandwich or that there's a nasty whiff coming from your brother's room.

It does something else REALLY important too.

It thinks.

All day every day – even when you're snoozing – your brain is working hard, imagining, remembering, dreaming and feeling.

Now do you understand why it's your body's HQ? Everything you do, think and feel comes from your brain. You'd be nothing without it!

HOW DOES YOUR BRAIN WORK?

To understand what's happening in your brain and how exactly it works, imagine that it consists of three sections:

- at the base is the "reptilian" or "primal" section, which keeps your vital organs working and puts you in survival mode if you feel threatened

- above that is the "mammal" or "emotional" section, which governs your emotional responses and connections

- the top part of your brain is known as the "thinking" section as it controls impulses and considers consequences

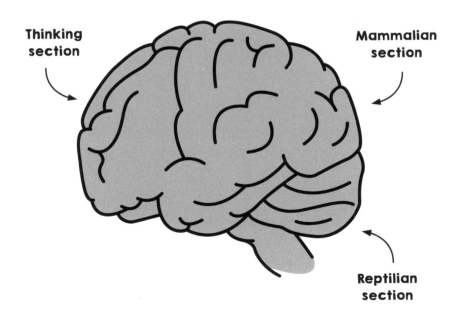

Thinking section

Mammalian section

Reptilian section

WHEN YOU THINK
ABOUT IT, THE BRAIN
IS ACTUALLY THE
MOST COMPLEX ORGAN
IN YOUR BODY.

DEMI LOVATO

EVERYTHING'S CHANGING

Look at some old baby pictures (aww, ickle you was SO cute) and it's clear to see how much you've grown since then.

Get this: by the age of six, your brain was already 90–95 per cent the size of an adult's brain. Yes, really! Since then, your brain has continued to develop – which is why you're probably now more adept at skills like reading, writing, tying your shoe laces and tidying your room (although possibly not that last one).

But your brain still needs heaps of remodelling in order for it to become a fully fledged adult brain. And, even though you can't see them, those important changes are happening *right now*.

The changes in that brain of yours are happening at a rapid rate but it's all a bit, well, topsy turvy.

During your pre-teen and teen years, the emotional section of your brain develops faster than the thinking section (the bit that tells you you're hungry or tired), which continues to change and develop in the way it works even as you go into your twenties.

This back-to-front brain development is the reason why you feel emotions *so* deeply right now. Big feelings can be hard to handle and a bit overwhelming, but that's where something called self-care comes in. Self-care is anything you do for yourself that makes you feel cared for, such as brushing your teeth and hair and going to bed at a reasonable time. (More on self-care in chapter three.)

Also, as your "thinking brain" is currently taking a back seat, you're more likely to make spur-of-the-moment, emotion-led decisions.

You know, impulsive stuff like dyeing your hair blue or partying with friends rather than studying for a test... the sorts of choices that grown-ups may, erm, struggle to get on board with!

THE EMOTIONS QUIZ

How well do you handle your emotions? Circle the answer that's most like you.

My moods are...

a) up and down depending on what's happening

b) pretty stable

c) all over the place

If someone's mean to me, I...

a) might get upset but try not to let it bother me

b) ignore it – who cares what they say?

c) burst into tears and snap back at them

When I argue with someone at home, I...

a) feel annoyed for a while but get over it

b) try to see it from their point of view

c) shout and stomp out

When I have a test looming, I...

a) get anxious

b) remind myself that nerves are natural

c) break down in panicky tears

Getting things wrong makes me feel...

a) embarrassed and cross

b) momentarily annoyed but, hey, everyone makes mistakes

c) mortified and devastated, like I'll never get over it

Results

Mostly a) Some situations get the better of you but generally you cope with life's ups and downs. Learning about self-care will boost your resilience.

Mostly b) You're one cool customer when it comes to your emotions... sure you're not a grown-up in disguise?! But remember that it's okay to not always be okay and when that happens – speak up.

Mostly c) Life's an emotional rollercoaster for you right now isn't it? Being super emosh is natural at your age, but OTT reactions can be exhausting. Learn about coping strategies and self-care in chapter three and how to ask for help in chapter five.

MY HAPPY LIST

Write down five things that make you feel all warm and fuzzy.
From best friends to fave hobbies, take some time to reflect on
what makes you tick.

1

2

3

4

5

MY NOT-SO-HAPPY LIST

Jot down anything in your life right now that doesn't give you a smiley vibe. Identifying upsetting situations, difficult challenges or even people who bring you down is an important first step in finding your way back to feeling happy.

1

2

3

4

5

LET'S TALK ABOUT HORMONES

Your feelings are caused by chemical messengers (hormones and neurotransmitters), which start in your brain and ping around your body in your bloodstream. Different hormones are responsible for different emotions, such as:

OXYTOCIN
– love, empathy, care, trust

DOPAMINE
– happiness, well-being, pleasure

ADRENALINE
– anger, worry, fear, anxiety

CORTISOL
– stress

DON'T RESIST CHANGE, EMBRACE IT

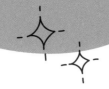

PUBERTY — WHAT'S HAPPENING TO MY BODY?

As a pre-teen or teen, it's not just your brain that's changing but your body too. For girls, you'll develop boobs and start having monthly periods. For boys, your testicles will drop and increase in size and your voice will start to "break" and deepen.

Your skin may change, becoming more oily, and you may develop zits or even acne.

Also, let's not forget body hair, which may start to sprout in the most unexpected of places, whether you're a boy or a girl.

There are some important hormones that trigger the physical changes brought on by puberty:

- Testosterone — known as the major male sex hormone but it's also found in smaller quantities in females

- Progesterone and oestrogen — referred to as the major female sex hormones but also found in smaller quantities in males

SO HOW DOES PUBERTY MAKE YOU FEEL?

Well, for a start, surges in testosterone, progesterone and oestrogen can affect your emotions, causing unexpected mood swings.

Also, during puberty, you might feel confused or sensitive about the way your changing body looks. You may no longer recognize yourself when you look in the mirror, or worry that your body is changing at a different rate to your friends' bodies.

For girls, periods can be tough. Premenstrual syndrome (PMS) can cause symptoms such as mood swings, tiredness, headaches, stomach aches and spots in the week leading up to your period.

When you're going through all this, try to remember that puberty won't last forever. Also, every single adult you know has gone through this life stage and survived it – pubes and all!

WHAT IS MENTAL HEALTH?

Physical health is easy to get your head around, right? It's all about how well your body works – your organs, muscles and bones – and whether you're suffering with any nasty bugs or infections.

Chances are, you know a bit about nurturing your physical health – eating well (not too much chocolate!), staying active (not spending too long on the sofa!) and taking general care of yourself.

But your mental health is harder to pin down, isn't it? You can't see it or mend it with a bandage, for starters.

It's still important though. Really important in fact.

Think of your mental health as a big umbrella covering a lot of important aspects of YOU. See why it's a big deal?

YOUR MENTAL HEALTH IS...

Your emotions

For instance, happy, grateful, hopeful, sad, angry, worried, envious, scared or anxious.

Your thoughts

Positive: "I'm having a really good day" or "I'm going to pass my exam."

Negative: "No one likes me!" or "I can't do all my schoolwork."

Your behaviour

Positive: smiling at your friends or saying thank you to someone who helps you.

Negative: bursting into tears or yelling when something goes wrong.

WHAT IF SOMETHING'S NOT RIGHT WITH YOUR MENTAL HEALTH?

Although you may not have given your mental health much thought until now, it's worth knowing that mental health issues in young people are a worldwide concern.

Research by the World Health Organization (WHO) has found that depression and anxiety are leading causes for ill-health in pre-teens and teens. Other issues – such as OCD, eating disorders and self-harm, along with many more – are also classed as mental health problems. These issues are explained in greater depth in chapter two.

Did you know that half of mental health conditions start by the age of 14? Sadly though, most of these go undiagnosed and untreated, which means countless young people are suffering in silence.

Poor mental health can drastically affect important areas of life such as school attendance. In turn, missing school can worsen your sense of isolation. It's a vicious circle, really. Sadly, if someone with poor mental health doesn't get help, it can lead to long-term problems, preventing them from enjoying life for years to come.

When it comes to getting help – either for you or for someone you know – it can be useful to know the early warning signs:

HOW'S YOUR MENTAL HEALTH?

When it comes to mental health issues, it's helpful to understand how you're feeling and what it might mean.

Right now, I feel...

a) a bit down

b) sad all the time

c) mostly okay

I feel worried...

a) quite a lot

b) constantly

c) occasionally about big stuff like exams

My sleep is...

a) patchy because I find it hard to relax

b) either non existent as I'm laying awake feeling awful OR I want to sleep all the time

c) just right for me

Around other people I feel...

a) okay depending on who I'm with

b) awful and just want to hide away on my own

c) happy and relaxed but I enjoy my own space too

Thinking about the future, I feel...

a)   scared – what if things don't work out?

b)   like there's no hope

c)   nervous but excited

Results

Mostly a) Life can sometimes get on top of you and that's perfectly normal but it's a good idea to share difficult feelings with someone you trust. Learning about self-care can be helpful – look at chapter three for tips.

Mostly b) You seem really sad and overwhelmed right now. Don't suffer in silence – talk to someone, whether that's a friend or relative or a professional like a teacher or doctor. There's further guidance in chapter five.

Mostly c) It looks like your mental health is in good shape but it's good to stay in tune with your feelings in case anything changes. Self-care will help keep your mind, body and soul in tip-top condition – take a look at chapter three.

WHAT IS NEURODIVERSITY?

Just as your fingerprints are unique, your brain is also one of a kind. No two people have a brain that is completely alike, not even identical twins.

However, the majority of people's brains still behave in a broadly similar way. If your brain functions similarly to the majority of other people's brains, it means you're "neurotypical".

A "neurodivergent" person's brain works differently, causing them to think (and possibly behave) differently.

Have you heard of autism, ADHD, dyslexia and dyspraxia? These neurological conditions cause a person to be "neurodivergent". Some people may have one condition or several.

Being neurodiverse isn't rare – it affects at least one in five people and cuts across race and gender. If you're showing signs, you can be assessed (see Further Resources, pages 152–155).

Signs of autism

- Finding it hard to express emotions
- Relying on rules and routines and struggling with change
- Difficulty understanding other people's emotions and forming friendships

Signs of ADHD

- Acting impulsively
- Constant fidgeting and talking
- Unable to concentrate

Signs of dyslexia

- Mixing up letters and numbers
- Inconsistent spelling and messy handwriting
- Reading and writing slowly

Signs of dyspraxia

- Balance and movement problems
- Problems with hand–eye coordination
- Fatigue

UNDERSTANDING YOUR SEXUAL ORIENTATION AND GENDER IDENTITY

During puberty, you'll become more aware of your sexuality and your sexual orientation. Sexual orientation is a grown-up term for people you fancy. You may be attracted to the opposite sex or the same sex or both.

Sexuality can be wide-ranging. For example, the term LGBTQ+ stands for lesbian, gay, bisexual, transgender, queer or more (see page 46 for more info).

Gender identity is separate from your sexual orientation and means how you feel about the gender you were assigned at birth.

Stereotypically, you will probably have been called female or male since you were born. While many people identify with this gender, you may be one of the many who don't.

People who identify as transgender or non-binary may choose to transition to a different gender and hormone treatments and surgery may be involved in this process.

AVOID THE COMPARISON TRAP

Ever heard the expression "Comparison is the thief of joy"?

It means that, by comparing yourself to others, whether that's friends or strangers IRL or online, you'll suck the fun out of life.

The truth is that you won't mature at the exact same rate as your peers and that goes for your body AND your brain. Just as your BFF (Best Friend Forever) may hit puberty before or after you, your brain development will follow a different schedule.

If you feel "out of sync", have been diagnosed as neurodivergent, are struggling with your mental health or are confused by your sexual orientation or gender identity, you may feel isolated.

But our uniqueness is what makes us wonderful! Try to cut yourself some slack and confide in people you trust. For more information on where to turn when times are tricky, look at chapter five.

CHAPTER TWO:

ALL ABOUT MENTAL HEALTH: AN A–Z

Knowledge is power, so it makes sense to be clued-up on the mental health issues experienced by pre-teens and teens. This chapter offers simple explanations to help you understand what you may be feeling.

TODAY, CHARTING YOUR OWN COURSE ISN'T JUST MORE NECESSARY THAN EVER BEFORE. IT'S ALSO MUCH EASIER — AND MUCH MORE FUN.

PiNK

ADDICTION

If someone is addicted to something – such as smoking, drinking alcohol or taking recreational drugs – they have no control over doing it, to the point where it may damage their health or well-being. Other addictions include:

- shopping – buying things you don't need or can't afford and then feeling guilty

- screen time – checking your phone constantly and feeling anxious when you can't access the internet or play video games

- work – obsessing over your studies to the detriment of other areas of life such as hobbies and seeing friends

- solvents – substance abuse isn't just about illegal drugs as you can become addicted to inhaling potentially fatal glue or aerosols

ANGER

Most of us experience anger sometimes. It's a normal human emotion, after all. But frequent angry outbursts can be damaging and frightening – not just for you but for the people around you. When you're angry, you may feel your muscles tense, your heart race and some people shout and start arguments or even self-harm when they're angry. You can learn ways to deal with anger such as mindfulness exercises and breathing techniques, which are explained in chapter three.

ANOREXIA

This eating disorder and mental health condition causes sufferers to over-exercise and limit their food to the point of starving their bodies. Anorexics may also have a distorted body image (body dysmorphic disorder, which is also known as BDD and is explained on page 42), which makes them believe that they're overweight even if they're actually very underweight. Although if you have anorexia, it may feel as though it's taken over your life, it is possible to recover from it – and the first step is to speak to a doctor.

ANXIETY

Feeling worried during difficult times, such as taking exams or starting a new school, is normal. But someone suffering constant anxiety about lots of things may have a mental health condition called generalized anxiety disorder (GAD).

Other anxiety disorders include obsessive compulsive disorder (OCD) and post-traumatic stress disorder (PTSD). Cognitive behavioural therapy (CBT) is a very effective way to treat anxiety; it's a type of psychotherapy that helps you challenge negative thought patterns about yourself or the world in general.

ATTENTION DEFICIT HYPERACTIVITY DISORDER (ADHD)

People with this neurological condition are more likely to suffer mental health problems. They may seem fidgety and over-talkative and can struggle to concentrate or finish tasks. They may also find it hard to go to sleep. The exact cause of ADHD isn't known but it can run in families. Generally, children with ADHD are now diagnosed at primary school age. Although there's no cure, treatments such as cognitive behavioural therapy (CBT – see page 39) can help.

BIPOLAR DISORDER

People with this mental health condition have extreme mood swings known as "mania" and "depression", which can last for weeks at a time.

During a manic phase, a person may feel happy, ambitious and creative but may also behave recklessly and struggle to eat or sleep. Depressive periods can make them feel worthless and despairing. Treatments for bipolar disorder include medication and talking therapies.

B

BODY DYSMORPHIC DISORDER (BDD)

This mental health condition is most common in teens and young adults. Someone with BDD has a skewed body image, which means that they may obsess over "flaws" in their appearance that no one else can see. For instance, they might mistakenly believe that they're fat when they're not at all. Sufferers often feel embarrassed to ask for help, but it's really important to get support as BDD can lead to other health issues such as eating problems (page 45) or eating disorders including anorexia (page 38) and bulimia (page 43).

B

BULIMIA

An eating disorder and mental health condition, bulimia can affect all age groups but is most common in teenagers. Bulimics binge eat (past the point of being full) and then try to avoid gaining weight by vomiting, using laxatives (to make them poo) or over-exercising. This is usually all done in secret.

As well as causing dangerous weight loss, it can lead to long-term damage of your body. The first step to recovery from any eating disorder is to speak to a health professional.

DEPRESSION

Most of us feel fed up at some point in our lives but clinical depression goes much deeper. If you're depressed, you feel sad for weeks or months.

You may lose interest in hobbies or friendships that previously made you happy, lose your appetite and either want to sleep constantly or struggle to sleep at all. Severe depression can lead to suicidal feelings (page 61) so it's really important that sufferers get support. With treatment, you can make a full recovery.

EATING PROBLEMS

An eating problem is any food-related difficulty that affects your life. You may find yourself restricting what you eat or feeling unable to stop overeating. Some people develop medically diagnosed eating disorders such as anorexia (page 38) or bulimia (page 43).

It's hard to admit to yourself or to anyone else that you have an eating problem, but seeking support is the first step to recovery. Speak to someone you trust such as a relative, teacher or your family doctor.

LGBTQ+ MENTAL HEALTH

If someone identifies as LGBTQ+, they may be lesbian, gay, bisexual, trans, intersex, non-binary, queer or define themselves in a different way. People who identify as LGBTQ+ are more prone to mental health issues, including low self-esteem, depression and anxiety. The reasons for this are complex but can partly be caused by discrimination they may face from people they know or complete strangers. Someone identifying as LGBTQ+ may also feel isolated because they feel "different" from other people.

If this is affecting you, talking to a counsellor or to trusted friends or family can be really useful in helping you feel less alone.

OBSESSIVE COMPULSIVE DISORDER (OCD)

Although obsessive compulsive disorder (OCD) is more common in adults, some teenagers develop symptoms. An obsession is a frequent unwanted thought and a compulsion is an action you feel you must do. For instance, you may worry that your hands aren't clean and find yourself repeatedly washing them until they're sore. OCD sufferers often feel ashamed and trapped by these private, inner feelings that are controlling their behaviour. But there is no need to feel like this – OCD is a recognized mental health condition and treatment such as cognitive behavioural therapy (CBT – see page 39) can really help.

PANIC ATTACKS

Panic attacks – when you feel sudden intense fear or panic without a particular trigger – can last between five and 30 minutes. Physical symptoms of a panic attack include:

- feeling faint or dizzy
- increased heart rate
- feeling sick
- sweating or trembling
- rapid breathing or shortness of breath
- crying

While panic attacks are frightening, they won't cause you any physical harm – although you may feel exhausted afterwards. But if you experience them repeatedly, there's a chance you might have panic disorder (a type of anxiety disorder) and would benefit from medical guidance.

P

PARANOIA

A type of ongoing irrational delusion (a mistaken belief), paranoia may make you believe that other people don't like you. Many of us experience mild paranoia at some point in our lives but these feelings are usually fleeting. However, a person with severe paranoia may believe that everyone is "out to get them", which can stop them forming close relationships. Paranoia isn't a mental health condition in itself but is a symptom linked to other mental health issues, such as schizophrenia (page 55) and psychosis (page 54).

P

PERSONALITY DISORDERS

Someone with a personality disorder might struggle with everyday life and the most common disorder, borderline personality disorder (BPD), causes impulsive behaviour and fear of abandonment. Support is available, however, and possible treatments include talking therapy and medication.

P

PHOBIAS

If you have an excessive fear of a situation or object that has lasted more than six months, you may have a phobia. Common phobias include arachnophobia (fear of spiders), acrophobia (fear of heights) and hemophobia (fear of blood).

Phobias may cause panic attacks (page 48) and can make life less enjoyable too, especially if they stop you doing things that you'd really like to do. Cognitive behavioural therapy (CBT – see page 39) can be a helpful way of addressing fear and moving forward.

P

POST-TRAUMATIC STRESS DISORDER (PTSD)

Trauma is an emotional response to a terrible experience – such as a serious accident – and it can be a mix of feelings such as fear, shock and panic. For some people, trauma subsides but one in three people who've endured a traumatic experience develop post-traumatic stress disorder (PTSD). Someone with this mental health condition may keep reliving their traumatic experience through nightmares or flashbacks, but therapy can be really helpful.

PREMENSTRUAL DYSPHORIC DISORDER (PMDD)

Sometimes known as "severe premenstrual syndrome", PMDD can cause really debilitating symptoms during your menstrual cycle each month. Emotional symptoms can include severe mood swings and even suicidal feelings (page 61), along with physical symptoms such as muscle and joint pains, headaches and sleep issues.

P

PSYCHOSIS

If someone has hallucinations (seeing and hearing things that aren't there) or delusions (believing things that aren't true) they may have psychosis. It can be a sign of mental health conditions such as schizophrenia (page 55), bipolar (page 41) or severe depression (page 44) and can also be triggered by a traumatic experience or drug and alcohol abuse. A person showing signs of psychosis needs urgent medical treatment.

SCHIZOPHRENIA

People with this severe long-term mental health condition may suffer a range of symptoms including hallucinations (seeing or hearing things that aren't real) and delusions (believing things that aren't true). This can make it hard for them to cope with daily life and they may become socially withdrawn. It's possible for schizophrenia to be treated with a combination of therapy and medication.

SELF-ESTEEM

Your own personal sense of self-worth is known as your self-esteem. If you have healthy self-esteem, you'll have positive feelings about yourself. But if you have low self-esteem, you may experience feelings of worthlessness and avoid certain situations for fear of failure. Ways of raising your self-esteem include focusing on your positive qualities, trying new challenges and, above all, being kind to yourself. The self-care tips in chapter three should help.

SELF-HARM

Intentionally hurting yourself – either by cutting, biting or some other method – is known as self-harm. Although self-harming can affect any age group, it is most common in teenagers. Some teenagers who self-harm say that they do it as a way of dealing with difficult situations or feelings, while others aren't sure what prompts them to hurt themselves. Some self-harmers may also have suicidal feelings (page 61) and if this is the case, it's really important to ask for help. Treatment for self-harm may first involve treating any physical wounds, such as cuts or bruises, followed by specialist talking therapy.

S

SKIN-PICKING DISORDER

If you find yourself unable to stop picking at your skin when you're anxious, stressed – or even when you're asleep – you may have this disorder, which is also known as dermatillomania or excoriation disorder. Excessive picking with your fingers, fingernails, teeth or tools such as tweezers can cause cuts, bruises and scars. You can help yourself by keeping your hands busy with a fidget toy or stress squeezer, but if you feel overwhelmed by your urge to pick, you may need to have a chat with a doctor for some guidance.

SLEEP PROBLEMS

You *should* get between eight and ten hours of sleep on school nights but not everyone finds snoozing simple. Some people struggle to drop off or wake up frequently. Poor quality sleep can negatively affect your state of mind, making you feel worn out and anxious. To help you relax, set a regular bedtime routine such as a bubble bath and a warm caffeine-free drink followed by reading a book or magazine before lights out. Try to avoid screens for at least an hour before bed. If you've tried all this and still can't sleep, have a chat with your doctor.

S

STRESS

Everyone feels stressed sometimes. Stress is a reaction to high pressure situations such as exams. Mild stress can actually be a good thing as it pushes you to *do* stuff (like revise!) but intense or long-term stress can cause health issues such as headaches, tummy aches, sleep issues, depression and anxiety. To stop yourself getting overwhelmed, break tasks into small manageable chunks and share how you're feeling with someone you trust.

S

SUICIDAL FEELINGS

Suicide is the act of someone taking their own life. If you're thinking that other people would be better off without you or if you're having thoughts about ending your life then you shouldn't have to struggle alone with those feelings. It's vital to tell someone that you're feeling so low and if you feel that you can't tell a loved one, there are free help organizations such as Samaritans in the USA or in the UK.

CHAPTER THREE:

SELF-CARE, AKA LOOKING AFTER MYSELF

Self-care isn't selfish or self-indulgent; it's about being kind to yourself so that you can weather life's storms. Whether you're tackling exam season, navigating tricky friendships or wondering about the importance of sleep and diet, by understanding your self-care needs, you can build an indestructible toolkit for dealing with difficult times.

SELF-CARE IS SUPER
IMPORTANT, ESPECIALLY
MAKING SURE YOUR MENTAL
HEALTH IS GOOD, BECAUSE
WE'RE ALL FIGURING
THIS OUT TOGETHER.

KAIA GERBER

UNDERSTAND WHAT SELF-CARE ACTUALLY IS

You've probably heard the word "resilience" – the ability to bounce back from difficult times. The best way to build resilience? Focusing on self-care.

Self-care means taking time to look after yourself so you stay in good shape – physically, mentally and emotionally. But it's no good asking your mates about their ideas of self-care because everyone's needs are personal. For one friend, a long bath will work wonders; another will swear by sticking on their favourite music and having a dance. There really is no one-size-fits-all approach. Also, your self-care needs will change depending on what's going on around you. For instance, heading into exam season, you'll need to prepare for the academic challenges ahead. But while it might be tempting to pull all-night revision cramming sessions, you'll only end up exhausted and likely to underperform.

Instead, it would be wiser to focus on resting between revision sessions and exams and eating slow-release energy foods to boost your concentration.

Makes sense doesn't it?

Well, you see, that's the beauty of self-care – it's not complicated!

Can't help feeling that you're not worthy of self-care? Well, STOP RIGHT THERE because every single one of us is, okay?

But make sure you understand the difference between self-care and self-indulgence. Self-care always has the "Future You" in mind. Self-indulgence, on the other hand, is generally reckless behaviour that is unlikely to have a positive impact long-term; completely ditching your revision notes in favour of Netflix binges for instance. It might be fun in the moment but Future You, who has to sit in that exam room, definitely won't appreciate it.

So be kind to yourself and recognize that life is about maintaining a balance.

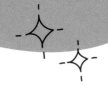

HOW TO DE-STRESS AND STAY CALM

Life is full of challenges when you're a pre-teen or teen. Perhaps you're overwhelmed by schoolwork or have argued with your BFF.

Also, don't forget all those pesky hormones flying around, affecting your mood.

While you can't stop yourself experiencing big emotions, you can learn to cope when the path gets bumpy. The key? Removing unnecessary stresses and creating a safe space where you can just "be". If that's your room, keep it tidy and uncluttered.

Create a mental health shelf – an easy-to-reach home for your favourite blanket, feel-good movies and books and stress squeezers. Perhaps mindful creativity is your thing – try the colour-in tracker pages in chapter four of this book for starters.

I HAVE LEARNED TO MANAGE
(ANXIETY) IN WAYS THAT
A LOT OF PEOPLE LEARN
TO MANAGE THINGS LIKE
BREATHING EXERCISES OR
DISTRACTING YOUR MIND,
AND MY HOBBIES HELP
DISTRACT ME FROM
BEING ANXIOUS.

MiLLiE BOBBY BROWN

THE SELF-CARE QUIZ

Let's take a look at how much you practise self-care with this quiz.

At the end of a hard day, I generally...

a) keep going over everything that went wrong and make myself feel even worse

b) try to put it out of my mind

c) chill out in my room and listen to my favourite happy music – it soon gets me smiling again

When I'm tired, I...

a) stay up late anyway, watching TV or pushing on with homework

b) go to bed a bit earlier than usual

c) have a relaxing bath, make a hot drink and then get into bed early to catch up on sleep

A friend says something that leaves me feeling upset, so I...

a) spend ages worrying what I have done to make them be so mean and wonder what to do to make it up to them

b) decide not to speak to them for a few days

c) remind myself that their behaviour is not my responsibility and spend time with friends who make me smile

If I do badly in a test, I...

a) get really upset and cross with myself

b) feel disappointed and vow to work harder next time

c) try not to let it get me down and make a proper revision plan for the next test – with plenty of time for work, plus relaxation time to avoid burn out

When I feel stressed, I...

a) find it difficult to calm down

b) try to ride it out and hope tomorrow is better

c) know that I need to look after myself by not panicking, eating well and doing things that relax me such as watching my favourite movie

Results

Mostly a) You give yourself a tough time when things don't go to plan and spend a fair bit of time feeling stressed. Know that you are totally worthy of self-care and would really benefit from the tips in this chapter.

Mostly b) You try to keep things balanced but can be a little hard on yourself. Self-care is key! Inspired by the tips in this book, think about your favourite feel-good pastimes and make a conscious effort to take care of yourself.

Mostly c) Congrats – self-care is second nature to you. There's always room for improvement though. Never forget that trying out new things is also a form of self-care if it makes you feel good!

HOW TO PLAN AND PREPARE FOR BIG DAYS

Do you have something BIG looming in the not-so-distant future?

It might be a fun event (party with your mates) or something not quite so fun (yep, you got it – another pesky exam).

Either way, it's completely normal to feel nervous about it all, whether you're worrying about what to wear or fretting that your revision notes aren't up to scratch. But avoid panicking and remember that you won't be the only one with jitters – far from it. In fact, why not tell a trusted friend that you're feeling anxious? They will probably admit to feeling the same.

Preparation is generally key here, so carve out plenty of revision time to minimize any exam worries or work out a party outfit well before the day to ensure you feel comfortable.

In the days leading up to your event, try confidence boosting "mirror affirmations" – a technique used in the past by famous names including the motivational author Louise Hay along with Winston Churchill and Salvador Dali. Looking in a mirror, give yourself a pep talk or repeat a mantra such as: "I am strong and self-assured and will do my best." Repeat this daily and you will hopefully feel your mindset shifting positively.

Also, try to remind yourself that, once you're at the party or in the exam room, your nerves will disappear because you'll be occupied. And remember that there's nothing like the buzz of knowing you've got through – and maybe possibly even enjoyed – that Big Thing you were dreading.

LITTLE THINGS THAT HELP ME RELAX

From listening to your favourite tunes to watching clouds in the sky, write down your top five chill-out methods – the simpler the better! Refer back to these ideas when you need some self-care.

1

2

3

4

5

MY HAPPY MEMORIES LIST

Whether it's that time you did well in a test or a special day spent with family or friends, jot down the memories that make you smile – and come back to this page whenever you need an instant mood boost.

GROUNDING AND MINDFULNESS EXERCISES FOR EXAMS

Exams can be overwhelming but the last thing you want is for your mind to wander.

Grounding is a mindfulness technique to help you stay "in the moment" and can keep you focused during times of stress.

Take a moment to focus your mind during revision sessions and exams with this simple grounding technique:

- **Step 1:** Pick up an object – the nearest pen or pencil is an obvious choice.

- **Step 2:** Hold it in your hand for a few moments.

- **Step 3:** Focus on how the object feels and how it looks, shutting out all external distractions around you.

- **Step 4:** Now that your mind is focused, return your concentration to your studies or your exam paper.

SELF-CARE ISN'T SELFISH

SLEEP

Yes, you may well feel like staying up until 3 a.m., reading or messing around on your phone. But the truth is that sleep is *really* important. In fact, you should get between eight and ten hours of snooze time every night, whether you've got school the next day or not.

Why? Well, as your body and brain are constantly growing and changing right now, you need nightly unbroken, deep sleep to fuel it all. Also, being tired can really affect your state of mind, making you feel strung out and anxious and risking you dropping off in class, which you should definitely avoid unless you enjoy detention.

But what if you find it tricky to drop off and actually stay asleep? Here are some simple ways to improve your sleep pattern...

- Establish a regular wind-down routine so your body recognizes that it's nearly bedtime

- Avoid screens for at least an hour before bed

- Have a relaxing bubble bath or shower

- Keep your bedroom clutter free

- Don't set your room temperature too high – 60–67°F (15.6–19.4°C) is ideal

- Play quiet, calming music

- Enjoy a soothing drink such as warm milk or decaffeinated fruit tea

- Put drops of essential oil on your pillow – lavender oil aids deep sleep

- Read a relaxing book (avoid nightmare-inducing horror stories!)

- Ensure that your room is dark – blackout curtains can help

- Use earplugs to block out noise

- Try a calming breathing technique – inhale slowly and deeply through your nose, keeping your shoulders relaxed. Exhale slowly through your mouth. As you blow out, purse your lips slightly, but keep your jaw relaxed. Repeat as necessary.

ADVICE ON EATING WELL

Self-care starts from within, so think about how the food you eat affects your body. A balanced diet gives you the nutrients you need to stay healthy. This means eating food and drink from all five food groups, which include:

- fruit and vegetables – at least five portions a day

- dairy or dairy alternatives such as oat or soya milk

- high fibre foods such as potatoes, rice, pasta or bread

- proteins such as beans, pulses, eggs, fish or meat

- unsaturated oils and spreads such as olive oil or peanut butter – in small amounts

You should also:

- drink plenty of fluids – at least six to eight glasses a day

- keep food and drinks that are high in sugar, fat or salt, such as sweets, crisps and fizzy soda, to a minimum

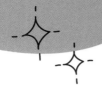

THE IMPORTANCE OF STAYING ACTIVE

Between the ages of five to 18, you should aim for at least an hour's moderate activity (such as walking to school or zipping around on your scooter or skateboard) each day. You should also do regular higher intensity activities such as playing football or dancing.

So why is it important to stay active? There are actually LOTS of reasons!

- It keeps you physically fit, working your muscles, lungs and heart, increasing your strength and helping you maintain a healthy weight.

- It's good for your mood because it stimulates chemicals in your brain (endorphins), leaving you feeling happier and more relaxed.

- It raises your self-esteem. Achieving a goal such as swimming ten lengths is a real confidence boost.

- It can be sociable too, as joining a sports team or club opens up your world to new like-minded buddies.

FRIENDSHIPS AND PEER GROUPS

You may have been inseparable with your BFFs since the start of primary school but once you start high school, your world opens up considerably. As part of a much bigger school community, you'll get to try exciting new subjects and activities – and with this opportunity comes the chance to make new mates too.

That doesn't mean that you should instantly shun your old pals in favour of a new crowd. But try not to worry too much if you find some of your longer-standing friendships drifting a little as you all immerse yourselves in your new world.

The truth is that it's normal and also totally understandable for friendships to change as you move from one life stage to another. So try not to over-analyse or force your current friendships too much. If you're destined to stay true friends for life then you will do.

On the flip side, if you never really gelled with the other kids at your first school, now's your chance to leave that behind and find the friends you always hoped you'd have.

Make the most of exploring new avenues for meeting other like-minded friends at high school – people who'll really "get" you and understand what you're all about.

And the best way to do this? Say yes to invitations, join clubs and go to meet-ups, whether they're virtual or face to face. Try to be patient because new friendships don't happen overnight, but just turning up and saying "hello" is the most important first step. And if you're nervous about it all, don't worry – the chances are that everyone else feels just as wobbly as you!

RECOGNIZING UNHEALTHY RELATIONSHIPS AND HOW TO DEAL WITH THEM

Relationships – romantic or otherwise – can be tricky and it's not always obvious when a friend isn't treating you well.

Maybe you have a pal who keeps using you as the butt of their jokes.

Perhaps someone in your life is pressuring you into something you're not sure about, such as cheating with school work or lying to your parents.

If any of this sounds familiar, ask yourself: "*Does this person have my best interests at heart?*"

If you can't honestly answer "yes", it might be time to take a step back.

Healthy relationships are built on mutual respect and understanding. Also, never forget the importance of self-care. If a friend is making you feel uneasy about something or bad about yourself, it's probably time to nurture your self-esteem by spending time with other people.

Above everything else, *be your own best friend.*

FIND YOUR TRIBE AND LOVE THEM HARD

MY FRIENDSHIP MANIFESTO

Write down your own personal rules for friendship, such as trust, a shared sense of humour and an understanding to always have each other's back. When you find friends who are all this and more to you, nurture them!

If someone is my BFF, they:

_____

_____

_____

_____

_____

_____

_____

_____

_____

MY FRIENDSHIP DON'TS

It's important to have firm boundaries when it comes to friendships and to not accept poor behaviour from other people. Golden rule – if someone makes you feel bad about yourself, you don't have to put up with it.

Behaviour I won't accept from other people:

_____

_____

_____

_____

_____

_____

_____

_____

HEALTHY SOCIAL MEDIA MANAGEMENT

You may think that there's no avoiding social media but, believe it or not, there was a time when it didn't exist and everyone managed fine – yes, really!

While social media can be fun, it can also open up a world that's hard to navigate. You may develop an unhealthy case of FOMO (Fear of Missing Out) if you see pics of friends hanging out together when you're stuck at home finishing coursework. Perhaps you feel anxious about sharing selfies and being judged by others.

Did you know that some experts describe overuse of social media as "self-harm"? It sounds dramatic but, actually, excessive use of social media can fuel mental health issues such as anxiety and depression.

Listen up and listen good: NEVER value your self-worth by likes or followers. Neither should you let anyone – people you know or strangers who slide into your DMs – intimidate or upset you online.

How does social media make you feel? If you find yourself getting panicky or sad as you scroll then it's doing you no favours.

Be brave and try turning off your devices for ten minutes, even if it feels strange. Build up to longer stints offline and turn off your phone well before bedtime.

Each morning, rather than reaching straight for your phone, spend a few moments thinking about what you're going to do with your day. After all, you can't enjoy any exciting opportunities coming your way if you're dwelling on stuff you've seen online.

CHAPTER FOUR:

MY MOODS

Mood trackers are a simple tool to help you map your emotions. Track your moods through the year with the 12 monthly trackers in this chapter, colouring in the most relevant emoji for each day. Do you notice any patterns to the way you feel? Once you notice a pattern for your moods and emotions, you may be able to predict those days when you're likely to need some extra TLC.

In this chapter, you can also take time to focus on other aspects of your life, by tracking your sleep patterns, food, exercise and water intake as well as completing other fill-in pages to get you thinking about self-care and a more positive mind set. The notes you make on these pages should give you a picture of where you're at with your moods and with your life habits in general.

So what are you waiting for? Get tracking!

TO ALL THOSE LIKE ME
WHO OVERSCHEDULE,
OVERTHINK, OVERWORK,
OVER-WORRY, AND OVER-
EVERYTHING, PLEASE
KNOW YOU'RE NOT ALONE.
WE DON'T TALK ENOUGH
ABOUT MENTAL HEALTH.

RYAN REYNOLDS

HOW DO YOU FEEL?

Write some words to describe how you feel now:

Write some words to describe how you'd like to feel:

WHAT WOULD YOU LIKE TO CHANGE?

Are there feelings you'd like to change? Write down some ideas to help you change negative feelings, such as getting more sleep, spending less time on social media or hanging out with friends who make you truly happy.

1

2

3

4

5

JANUARY MOOD TRACKER

Track your moods this month by colouring in the most relevant emoji for each day. At the end of the month, do you notice any patterns to the way you feel?

1	☺	😐	☹	😠	😖		17	☺	😐	☹	😠	😖
2	☺	😐	☹	😠	😖		18	☺	😐	☹	😠	😖
3	☺	😐	☹	😠	😖		19	☺	😐	☹	😠	😖
4	☺	😐	☹	😠	😖		20	☺	😐	☹	😠	😖
5	☺	😐	☹	😠	😖		21	☺	😐	☹	😠	😖
6	☺	😐	☹	😠	😖		22	☺	😐	☹	😠	😖
7	☺	😐	☹	😠	😖		23	☺	😐	☹	😠	😖
8	☺	😐	☹	😠	😖		24	☺	😐	☹	😠	😖
9	☺	😐	☹	😠	😖		25	☺	😐	☹	😠	😖
10	☺	😐	☹	😠	😖		26	☺	😐	☹	😠	😖
11	☺	😐	☹	😠	😖		27	☺	😐	☹	😠	😖
12	☺	😐	☹	😠	😖		28	☺	😐	☹	😠	😖
13	☺	😐	☹	😠	😖		29	☺	😐	☹	😠	😖
14	☺	😐	☹	😠	😖		30	☺	😐	☹	😠	😖
15	☺	😐	☹	😠	😖		31	☺	😐	☹	😠	😖
16	☺	😐	☹	😠	😖							

FOOD TRACKER

Track your food for a week – any week will do! Colour in each section of the plate. At the end of the week, look at the colours on your plate – how healthy is your diet and what changes could you make? For advice on eating well, go to page 78.

☐ **Very healthy**

☐ **Mostly healthy**

☐ **A little unhealthy**

☐ **Very unhealthy**

FEBRUARY MOOD TRACKER

Track your moods this month by colouring in the most relevant emoji for each day. At the end of the month, do you notice any patterns to the way you feel?

Day	Moods		Day	Moods
1	☺ ☺ ☹ 😣 ☺		16	☺ ☺ ☹ 😣 ☺
2	☺ ☺ ☹ 😣 ☺		17	☺ ☺ ☹ 😣 ☺
3	☺ ☺ ☹ 😣 ☺		18	☺ ☺ ☹ 😣 ☺
4	☺ ☺ ☹ 😣 ☺		19	☺ ☺ ☹ 😣 ☺
5	☺ ☺ ☹ 😣 ☺		20	☺ ☺ ☹ 😣 ☺
6	☺ ☺ ☹ 😣 ☺		21	☺ ☺ ☹ 😣 ☺
7	☺ ☺ ☹ 😣 ☺		22	☺ ☺ ☹ 😣 ☺
8	☺ ☺ ☹ 😣 ☺		23	☺ ☺ ☹ 😣 ☺
9	☺ ☺ ☹ 😣 ☺		24	☺ ☺ ☹ 😣 ☺
10	☺ ☺ ☹ 😣 ☺		25	☺ ☺ ☹ 😣 ☺
11	☺ ☺ ☹ 😣 ☺		26	☺ ☺ ☹ 😣 ☺
12	☺ ☺ ☹ 😣 ☺		27	☺ ☺ ☹ 😣 ☺
13	☺ ☺ ☹ 😣 ☺		28	☺ ☺ ☹ 😣 ☺
14	☺ ☺ ☹ 😣 ☺		29	☺ ☺ ☹ 😣 ☺
15	☺ ☺ ☹ 😣 ☺			

WATER TRACKER

Choose a week and colour in a drop every time you drink a glass of water.

Monday	◊ ◊ ◊ ◊ ◊ ◊ ◊ ◊
Tuesday	◊ ◊ ◊ ◊ ◊ ◊ ◊ ◊
Wednesday	◊ ◊ ◊ ◊ ◊ ◊ ◊ ◊
Thursday	◊ ◊ ◊ ◊ ◊ ◊ ◊ ◊
Friday	◊ ◊ ◊ ◊ ◊ ◊ ◊ ◊
Saturday	◊ ◊ ◊ ◊ ◊ ◊ ◊ ◊
Sunday	◊ ◊ ◊ ◊ ◊ ◊ ◊ ◊

At your age, you should drink around 1.5 litres of water a day. Of course it depends how big the glass you're using is, but try to aim for six to eight glasses of water a day to keep you hydrated and thinking clearly. Bear in mind that being even slightly dehydrated can lead to moodiness, lack of concentration, headaches and tiredness, so your water intake is really important.

ONE-DAY MOOD TRACKER

Pick any day of the month and colour in one section per hour to get a picture of your moods during the day.

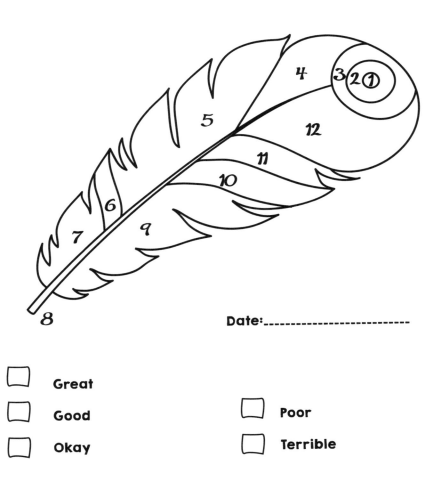

Date:_____

☐ **Great**

☐ **Good**

☐ **Okay**

☐ **Poor**

☐ **Terrible**

THE MINUTE YOU
LEARN TO LOVE
YOURSELF, YOU
WON'T WANT TO
BE ANYONE ELSE.

RiHANNA

MARCH MOOD TRACKER

Track your moods this month by colouring in the most relevant emoji for each day. At the end of the month, do you notice any patterns to the way you feel?

Day						Day					
1	🙂	😐	🙁	😠	😦	17	🙂	😐	🙁	😠	😦
2	🙂	😐	🙁	😠	😦	18	🙂	😐	🙁	😠	😦
3	🙂	😐	🙁	😠	😦	19	🙂	😐	🙁	😠	😦
4	🙂	😐	🙁	😠	😦	20	🙂	😐	🙁	😠	😦
5	🙂	😐	🙁	😠	😦	21	🙂	😐	🙁	😠	😦
6	🙂	😐	🙁	😠	😦	22	🙂	😐	🙁	😠	😦
7	🙂	😐	🙁	😠	😦	23	🙂	😐	🙁	😠	😦
8	🙂	😐	🙁	😠	😦	24	🙂	😐	🙁	😠	😦
9	🙂	😐	🙁	😠	😦	25	🙂	😐	🙁	😠	😦
10	🙂	😐	🙁	😠	😦	26	🙂	😐	🙁	😠	😦
11	🙂	😐	🙁	😠	😦	27	🙂	😐	🙁	😠	😦
12	🙂	😐	🙁	😠	😦	28	🙂	😐	🙁	😠	😦
13	🙂	😐	🙁	😠	😦	29	🙂	😐	🙁	😠	😦
14	🙂	😐	🙁	😠	😦	30	🙂	😐	🙁	😠	😦
15	🙂	😐	🙁	😠	😦	31	🙂	😐	🙁	😠	😦
16	🙂	😐	🙁	😠	😦						

APRIL MOOD TRACKER

Track your moods this month by colouring in the most relevant emoji for each day. At the end of the month, do you notice any patterns to the way you feel?

Day	Moods	Day	Moods
1	☺ ☺ ☹ 😠 😖	16	☺ ☺ ☹ 😠 😖
2	☺ ☺ ☹ 😠 😖	17	☺ ☺ ☹ 😠 😖
3	☺ ☺ ☹ 😠 😖	18	☺ ☺ ☹ 😠 😖
4	☺ ☺ ☹ 😠 😖	19	☺ ☺ ☹ 😠 😖
5	☺ ☺ ☹ 😠 😖	20	☺ ☺ ☹ 😠 😖
6	☺ ☺ ☹ 😠 😖	21	☺ ☺ ☹ 😠 😖
7	☺ ☺ ☹ 😠 😖	22	☺ ☺ ☹ 😠 😖
8	☺ ☺ ☹ 😠 😖	23	☺ ☺ ☹ 😠 😖
9	☺ ☺ ☹ 😠 😖	24	☺ ☺ ☹ 😠 😖
10	☺ ☺ ☹ 😠 😖	25	☺ ☺ ☹ 😠 😖
11	☺ ☺ ☹ 😠 😖	26	☺ ☺ ☹ 😠 😖
12	☺ ☺ ☹ 😠 😖	27	☺ ☺ ☹ 😠 😖
13	☺ ☺ ☹ 😠 😖	28	☺ ☺ ☹ 😠 😖
14	☺ ☺ ☹ 😠 😖	29	☺ ☺ ☹ 😠 😖
15	☺ ☺ ☹ 😠 😖	30	☺ ☺ ☹ 😠 😖

GRATITUDE LIST

Jot down ten things in your life that you are grateful for, even the tiniest of things that make you smile. Whenever you're feeling low and need a pick-me-up, take a moment to reflect on this list.

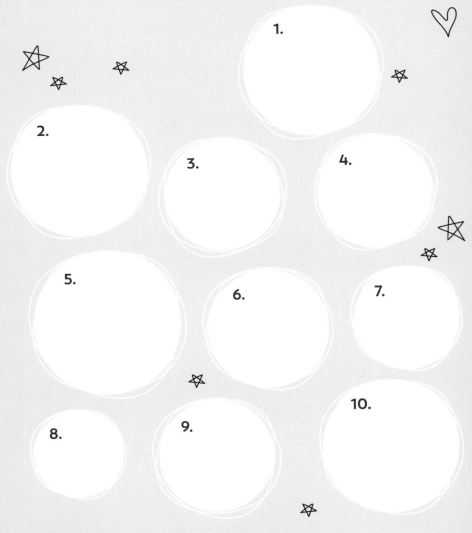

1.

2.

3.

4.

5.

6.

7.

8.

9.

10.

MAY MOOD TRACKER

Track your moods this month by colouring in the most relevant emoji for each day. At the end of the month, do you notice any patterns to the way you feel?

Day	Moods		Day	Moods
1	☺ 😐 ☹ 😡 😖		17	☺ 😐 ☹ 😡 😖
2	☺ 😐 ☹ 😡 😖		18	☺ 😐 ☹ 😡 😖
3	☺ 😐 ☹ 😡 😖		19	☺ 😐 ☹ 😡 😖
4	☺ 😐 ☹ 😡 😖		20	☺ 😐 ☹ 😡 😖
5	☺ 😐 ☹ 😡 😖		21	☺ 😐 ☹ 😡 😖
6	☺ 😐 ☹ 😡 😖		22	☺ 😐 ☹ 😡 😖
7	☺ 😐 ☹ 😡 😖		23	☺ 😐 ☹ 😡 😖
8	☺ 😐 ☹ 😡 😖		24	☺ 😐 ☹ 😡 😖
9	☺ 😐 ☹ 😡 😖		25	☺ 😐 ☹ 😡 😖
10	☺ 😐 ☹ 😡 😖		26	☺ 😐 ☹ 😡 😖
11	☺ 😐 ☹ 😡 😖		27	☺ 😐 ☹ 😡 😖
12	☺ 😐 ☹ 😡 😖		28	☺ 😐 ☹ 😡 😖
13	☺ 😐 ☹ 😡 😖		29	☺ 😐 ☹ 😡 😖
14	☺ 😐 ☹ 😡 😖		30	☺ 😐 ☹ 😡 😖
15	☺ 😐 ☹ 😡 😖		31	☺ 😐 ☹ 😡 😖
16	☺ 😐 ☹ 😡 😖			

JUNE MOOD TRACKER

Track your moods this month by colouring in the most relevant emoji for each day. At the end of the month, do you notice any patterns to the way you feel?

1	☺ ☺ ☹ ☹ ☹					16	☺ ☺ ☹ ☹ ☹				
2	☺ ☺ ☹ ☹ ☹					17	☺ ☺ ☹ ☹ ☹				
3	☺ ☺ ☹ ☹ ☹					18	☺ ☺ ☹ ☹ ☹				
4	☺ ☺ ☹ ☹ ☹					19	☺ ☺ ☹ ☹ ☹				
5	☺ ☺ ☹ ☹ ☹					20	☺ ☺ ☹ ☹ ☹				
6	☺ ☺ ☹ ☹ ☹					21	☺ ☺ ☹ ☹ ☹				
7	☺ ☺ ☹ ☹ ☹					22	☺ ☺ ☹ ☹ ☹				
8	☺ ☺ ☹ ☹ ☹					23	☺ ☺ ☹ ☹ ☹				
9	☺ ☺ ☹ ☹ ☹					24	☺ ☺ ☹ ☹ ☹				
10	☺ ☺ ☹ ☹ ☹					25	☺ ☺ ☹ ☹ ☹				
11	☺ ☺ ☹ ☹ ☹					26	☺ ☺ ☹ ☹ ☹				
12	☺ ☺ ☹ ☹ ☹					27	☺ ☺ ☹ ☹ ☹				
13	☺ ☺ ☹ ☹ ☹					28	☺ ☺ ☹ ☹ ☹				
14	☺ ☺ ☹ ☹ ☹					29	☺ ☺ ☹ ☹ ☹				
15	☺ ☺ ☹ ☹ ☹					30	☺ ☺ ☹ ☹ ☹				

FEEL-BETTER FIXES

Think about five things that always make you feel better when you're down – whether it's your snuggly duvet, favourite movie or a yummy edible treat. Keep a note of them here so that you have a go-to comfort list to lift your spirits on rubbish days.

1

2

3

4

5

SLEEP TRACKER

Choose a week and colour in a slice of the moon for every night to indicate how much sleep you got. If you have lots of slices of moon indicating that you got less than seven or eight hours, it might be time to have a think about your sleep routine. Remember that lack of sleep can really affect your mood. For more tips on sleep, look at pages 59, 76 and 77.

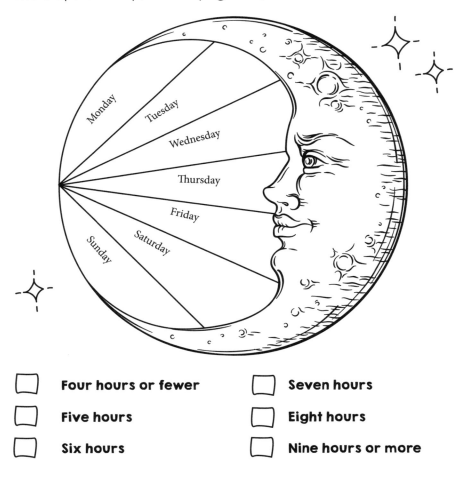

☐ Four hours or fewer   ☐ Seven hours

☐ Five hours   ☐ Eight hours

☐ Six hours   ☐ Nine hours or more

JULY MOOD TRACKER

Track your moods this month by colouring in the most relevant emoji for each day. At the end of the month, do you notice any patterns to the way you feel?

Day	Moods		Day	Moods
1	☺ ☺ ☹ 😣 ☺		17	☺ ☺ ☹ 😣 ☺
2	☺ ☺ ☹ 😣 ☺		18	☺ ☺ ☹ 😣 ☺
3	☺ ☺ ☹ 😣 ☺		19	☺ ☺ ☹ 😣 ☺
4	☺ ☺ ☹ 😣 ☺		20	☺ ☺ ☹ 😣 ☺
5	☺ ☺ ☹ 😣 ☺		21	☺ ☺ ☹ 😣 ☺
6	☺ ☺ ☹ 😣 ☺		22	☺ ☺ ☹ 😣 ☺
7	☺ ☺ ☹ 😣 ☺		23	☺ ☺ ☹ 😣 ☺
8	☺ ☺ ☹ 😣 ☺		24	☺ ☺ ☹ 😣 ☺
9	☺ ☺ ☹ 😣 ☺		25	☺ ☺ ☹ 😣 ☺
10	☺ ☺ ☹ 😣 ☺		26	☺ ☺ ☹ 😣 ☺
11	☺ ☺ ☹ 😣 ☺		27	☺ ☺ ☹ 😣 ☺
12	☺ ☺ ☹ 😣 ☺		28	☺ ☺ ☹ 😣 ☺
13	☺ ☺ ☹ 😣 ☺		29	☺ ☺ ☹ 😣 ☺
14	☺ ☺ ☹ 😣 ☺		30	☺ ☺ ☹ 😣 ☺
15	☺ ☺ ☹ 😣 ☺		31	☺ ☺ ☹ 😣 ☺
16	☺ ☺ ☹ 😣 ☺			

SELF-CARE TRACKER

Choose any week and fill in a heart every time you practise self-care – have a look at chapter three if you need some self-care inspiration, but as a general rule, if it makes you feel looked after and boosts your well-being, it's self-care!

Monday	♡ ♡ ♡ ♡
Tuesday	♡ ♡ ♡ ♡
Wednesday	♡ ♡ ♡ ♡
Thursday	♡ ♡ ♡ ♡
Friday	♡ ♡ ♡ ♡
Saturday	♡ ♡ ♡ ♡
Sunday	♡ ♡ ♡ ♡

At the end of the week, take note of how often you practise self-care. Are you doing enough to take care of yourself?

PUT YOURSELF RIGHT AT THE TOP OF YOUR TO-DO LIST

SELF-CARE CHECKLIST

Knowing how to look after yourself is all-important. Write down some of your favourite self-care techniques here, whether that's sinking into a bubble bath, heading out for a walk or something else that gives you a lift. Keep referring to this page so that you don't forget to fit in some self-care every day.

1

2

3

4

5

Track your moods this month by colouring in the most relevant emoji for each day. At the end of the month, do you notice any patterns to the way you feel?

1	☺ ☺ ☺ ☺ ☺	17	☺ ☺ ☺ ☺ ☺
2	☺ ☺ ☺ ☺ ☺	18	☺ ☺ ☺ ☺ ☺
3	☺ ☺ ☺ ☺ ☺	19	☺ ☺ ☺ ☺ ☺
4	☺ ☺ ☺ ☺ ☺	20	☺ ☺ ☺ ☺ ☺
5	☺ ☺ ☺ ☺ ☺	21	☺ ☺ ☺ ☺ ☺
6	☺ ☺ ☺ ☺ ☺	22	☺ ☺ ☺ ☺ ☺
7	☺ ☺ ☺ ☺ ☺	23	☺ ☺ ☺ ☺ ☺
8	☺ ☺ ☺ ☺ ☺	24	☺ ☺ ☺ ☺ ☺
9	☺ ☺ ☺ ☺ ☺	25	☺ ☺ ☺ ☺ ☺
10	☺ ☺ ☺ ☺ ☺	26	☺ ☺ ☺ ☺ ☺
11	☺ ☺ ☺ ☺ ☺	27	☺ ☺ ☺ ☺ ☺
12	☺ ☺ ☺ ☺ ☺	28	☺ ☺ ☺ ☺ ☺
13	☺ ☺ ☺ ☺ ☺	29	☺ ☺ ☺ ☺ ☺
14	☺ ☺ ☺ ☺ ☺	30	☺ ☺ ☺ ☺ ☺
15	☺ ☺ ☺ ☺ ☺	31	☺ ☺ ☺ ☺ ☺
16	☺ ☺ ☺ ☺ ☺		

GLASS HALF FULL?

Colour in how you felt today on the glass below.

Fantastic

Great

Good

Average

Down

Awful

How much of the glass is coloured in? What went right and what went wrong? How can you make changes for next week?

SEPTEMBER MOOD TRACKER

Track your moods this month by colouring in the most relevant emoji for each day. At the end of the month, do you notice any patterns to the way you feel?

Day	Moods		Day	Moods
1	☺ ☺ ☹ ☹ ☹		16	☺ ☺ ☹ ☹ ☹
2	☺ ☺ ☹ ☹ ☹		17	☺ ☺ ☹ ☹ ☹
3	☺ ☺ ☹ ☹ ☹		18	☺ ☺ ☹ ☹ ☹
4	☺ ☺ ☹ ☹ ☹		19	☺ ☺ ☹ ☹ ☹
5	☺ ☺ ☹ ☹ ☹		20	☺ ☺ ☹ ☹ ☹
6	☺ ☺ ☹ ☹ ☹		21	☺ ☺ ☹ ☹ ☹
7	☺ ☺ ☹ ☹ ☹		22	☺ ☺ ☹ ☹ ☹
8	☺ ☺ ☹ ☹ ☹		23	☺ ☺ ☹ ☹ ☹
9	☺ ☺ ☹ ☹ ☹		24	☺ ☺ ☹ ☹ ☹
10	☺ ☺ ☹ ☹ ☹		25	☺ ☺ ☹ ☹ ☹
11	☺ ☺ ☹ ☹ ☹		26	☺ ☺ ☹ ☹ ☹
12	☺ ☺ ☹ ☹ ☹		27	☺ ☺ ☹ ☹ ☹
13	☺ ☺ ☹ ☹ ☹		28	☺ ☺ ☹ ☹ ☹
14	☺ ☺ ☹ ☹ ☹		29	☺ ☺ ☹ ☹ ☹
15	☺ ☺ ☹ ☹ ☹		30	☺ ☺ ☹ ☹ ☹

Track your moods this month by colouring in the most relevant emoji for each day. At the end of the month, do you notice any patterns to the way you feel?

Day		Day	
1	🙂 😐 ☹️ 😠 😖	17	🙂 😐 ☹️ 😠 😖
2	🙂 😐 ☹️ 😠 😖	18	🙂 😐 ☹️ 😠 😖
3	🙂 😐 ☹️ 😠 😖	19	🙂 😐 ☹️ 😠 😖
4	🙂 😐 ☹️ 😠 😖	20	🙂 😐 ☹️ 😠 😖
5	🙂 😐 ☹️ 😠 😖	21	🙂 😐 ☹️ 😠 😖
6	🙂 😐 ☹️ 😠 😖	22	🙂 😐 ☹️ 😠 😖
7	🙂 😐 ☹️ 😠 😖	23	🙂 😐 ☹️ 😠 😖
8	🙂 😐 ☹️ 😠 😖	24	🙂 😐 ☹️ 😠 😖
9	🙂 😐 ☹️ 😠 😖	25	🙂 😐 ☹️ 😠 😖
10	🙂 😐 ☹️ 😠 😖	26	🙂 😐 ☹️ 😠 😖
11	🙂 😐 ☹️ 😠 😖	27	🙂 😐 ☹️ 😠 😖
12	🙂 😐 ☹️ 😠 😖	28	🙂 😐 ☹️ 😠 😖
13	🙂 😐 ☹️ 😠 😖	29	🙂 😐 ☹️ 😠 😖
14	🙂 😐 ☹️ 😠 😖	30	🙂 😐 ☹️ 😠 😖
15	🙂 😐 ☹️ 😠 😖	31	🙂 😐 ☹️ 😠 😖
16	🙂 😐 ☹️ 😠 😖		

EXERCISE TRACKER

Choose a week and colour in a droplet for every five minutes of activity you do.

Monday	🜄 🜄 🜄 🜄 🜄 🜄 🜄 🜄
Tuesday	🜄 🜄 🜄 🜄 🜄 🜄 🜄 🜄
Wednesday	🜄 🜄 🜄 🜄 🜄 🜄 🜄 🜄
Thursday	🜄 🜄 🜄 🜄 🜄 🜄 🜄 🜄
Friday	🜄 🜄 🜄 🜄 🜄 🜄 🜄 🜄
Saturday	🜄 🜄 🜄 🜄 🜄 🜄 🜄 🜄
Sunday	🜄 🜄 🜄 🜄 🜄 🜄 🜄 🜄

It's important to try to make time for at least 60 minutes of physical activity a day, whether that's walking briskly or cycling, zipping around on your scooter or having a dance to your favourite songs. For advice on exercise, go to page 79.

NOVEMBER MOOD TRACKER

Track your moods this month by colouring in the most relevant emoji for each day. At the end of the month, do you notice any patterns to the way you feel?

1	☺ ☺ ☹ ☹ ☺	16	☺ ☺ ☹ ☹ ☺
2	☺ ☺ ☹ ☹ ☺	17	☺ ☺ ☹ ☹ ☺
3	☺ ☺ ☹ ☹ ☺	18	☺ ☺ ☹ ☹ ☺
4	☺ ☺ ☹ ☹ ☺	19	☺ ☺ ☹ ☹ ☺
5	☺ ☺ ☹ ☹ ☺	20	☺ ☺ ☹ ☹ ☺
6	☺ ☺ ☹ ☹ ☺	21	☺ ☺ ☹ ☹ ☺
7	☺ ☺ ☹ ☹ ☺	22	☺ ☺ ☹ ☹ ☺
8	☺ ☺ ☹ ☹ ☺	23	☺ ☺ ☹ ☹ ☺
9	☺ ☺ ☹ ☹ ☺	24	☺ ☺ ☹ ☹ ☺
10	☺ ☺ ☹ ☹ ☺	25	☺ ☺ ☹ ☹ ☺
11	☺ ☺ ☹ ☹ ☺	26	☺ ☺ ☹ ☹ ☺
12	☺ ☺ ☹ ☹ ☺	27	☺ ☺ ☹ ☹ ☺
13	☺ ☺ ☹ ☹ ☺	28	☺ ☺ ☹ ☹ ☺
14	☺ ☺ ☹ ☹ ☺	29	☺ ☺ ☹ ☹ ☺
15	☺ ☺ ☹ ☹ ☺	30	☺ ☺ ☹ ☹ ☺

DIFFICULT ROADS CAN LEAD TO BEAUTIFUL DESTINATIONS

ONE-DAY MOOD TRACKER

Pick any day of the month and colour in the shell, one section per hour, to get a snapshot of your mood over the course of a day. Are there any particular times when you feel a bit down? By identifying moments that are difficult, you could work out triggers and solutions. For example, if you feel a bit down mid-afternoon, you may just need a quick, healthy snack to give you a boost.

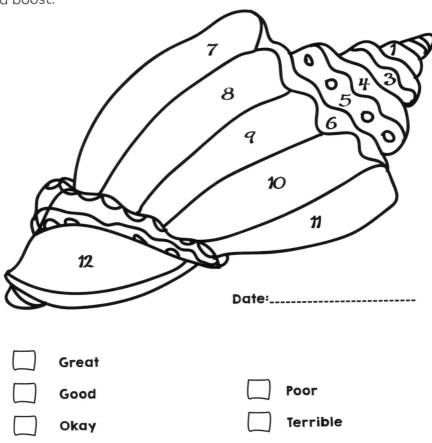

Date:_____

	Great		
	Good		Poor
	Okay		Terrible

DECEMBER MOOD TRACKER

Track your moods this month by colouring in the most relevant emoji for each day. At the end of the month, do you notice any patterns to the way you feel?

1	☺ ☺ ☹ 😠 😵	17	☺ ☺ ☹ 😠 😵
2	☺ ☺ ☹ 😠 😵	18	☺ ☺ ☹ 😠 😵
3	☺ ☺ ☹ 😠 😵	19	☺ ☺ ☹ 😠 😵
4	☺ ☺ ☹ 😠 😵	20	☺ ☺ ☹ 😠 😵
5	☺ ☺ ☹ 😠 😵	21	☺ ☺ ☹ 😠 😵
6	☺ ☺ ☹ 😠 😵	22	☺ ☺ ☹ 😠 😵
7	☺ ☺ ☹ 😠 😵	23	☺ ☺ ☹ 😠 😵
8	☺ ☺ ☹ 😠 😵	24	☺ ☺ ☹ 😠 😵
9	☺ ☺ ☹ 😠 😵	25	☺ ☺ ☹ 😠 😵
10	☺ ☺ ☹ 😠 😵	26	☺ ☺ ☹ 😠 😵
11	☺ ☺ ☹ 😠 😵	27	☺ ☺ ☹ 😠 😵
12	☺ ☺ ☹ 😠 😵	28	☺ ☺ ☹ 😠 😵
13	☺ ☺ ☹ 😠 😵	29	☺ ☺ ☹ 😠 😵
14	☺ ☺ ☹ 😠 😵	30	☺ ☺ ☹ 😠 😵
15	☺ ☺ ☹ 😠 😵	31	☺ ☺ ☹ 😠 😵
16	☺ ☺ ☹ 😠 😵		

MY TRACKER SUMMARY

Looking back at this chapter will give you a clearer picture of your moods and other areas of your life. Fill in this section to give you an idea of your life balance – and what you may need to work on.

My moods

How often do I feel sad or worried and is there a pattern to my mood changes?

_____

_____

_____

Sleep

Do I get enough sleep each night?

_____

_____

_____

Exercise

Do I get enough daily exercise?

_____

_____

_____

My diet

Do I usually eat my five-a-day?

_____

_____

_____

Water

Do I drink enough water each day?

_____

_____

_____

What I need to work on

Jot down some ideas for areas of your life that you'd like to improve on, whether that's aiming for more exercise and a healthier diet or putting together a self-care package to help you cope with challenging times.

_____

_____

_____

_____

_____

_____

_____

CHAPTER FIVE:

WHO CAN HELP ME?

If you have a problem or are worried about something in your life, it's important to know that you don't need to cope alone. There are lots of people out there who want to help you. This chapter explains how to find them and what happens when you ask for help.

IF YOU'RE
AFRAID
TO ASK
FOR HELP,
DON'T BE.

ARIANA GRANDE

DON'T SUFFER IN SILENCE

First thing's first, no one should ever have to suffer in silence – and that includes you, okay?

If something is bothering you or you're worried about the way you're feeling, it's important to talk to someone you trust. There's a reason why that old saying "A problem shared is a problem halved" is so well known; it's because it's true!

Problems and worries can seem so much more serious when you're keeping them to yourself. You may well find that once you confide in someone you trust, you'll feel much better and less "weighed down".

Even if that person can't give you the exact help you need, they will hopefully be able to steer you in the right direction.

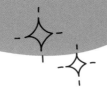

GETTING HELP IF YOU'RE BEING BULLIED

If someone is picking on you or making you feel sad or scared or ashamed of who you are, listen up. This is not your fault. The only person at fault in this situation is the bully.

Perhaps someone is sending you nasty messages online, which is known as cyber bullying. Whatever form it takes, bullying is abuse and it's wrong.

Quite simply, if you're being negatively affected by someone else's behaviour towards you, then it's important to seek help from someone you trust, whether that person is a good friend (who isn't involved in the bullying), your parent or guardian or a teacher at school.

KNOW WHO YOU CAN TRUST

It's good to recognize the people in your life who you can go to when you have a problem. Your "trusted people" could include any of the following:

- Your best friend

- Your sibling

- Your parent, guardian or grandparent

- Another relative

- Your teacher

- Your school nurse

- Your doctor

- Someone else in authority such as a social worker

Bear in mind that although it's great to share your problem with someone your own age, they may not be able to do much other than listen. If possible, go to an adult you trust. If you're nervous about doing this, you could ask your friend or sibling to go with you for support.

WHEN PEOPLE ASK
ME WHAT I'D SAY TO
SOMEBODY LOOKING
FOR ADVICE ON
MENTAL HEALTH, THE
ONLY THING I CAN SAY
IS PATIENCE. I HAD
PATIENCE WITH MYSELF.

BILLIE EILISH

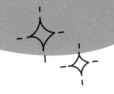

WHO CAN I TRUST?

Make a list of people you could share your feelings and worries with.

_____

_____

_____

_____

_____

_____

_____

_____

_____

_____

_____

_____

_____

_____

WHAT DO I WANT TO SHARE?

Jot down some ideas of what you'd like to talk about with your trusted person or people.

1

2

3

4

5

GETTING PROFESSIONAL HELP

Problems can't always be solved simply by talking with someone you trust and sometimes you might benefit from extra support. Perhaps you're experiencing emotional difficulties or are showing signs of neurodiversity (see pages 30–31).

The thought of speaking to a professional such as a doctor or counsellor may scare you, but remember that these people *want* to help.

So who might you see? Well, there are lots of different professional people you may see, depending on the issue you need help with. Some are health professionals; others work in social care or education.

These include:

- Your doctor – medical doctor treating the local community

- Paediatrician – doctor specializing in treating children and teenagers

- Nurse – care-giver who works in a hospital or clinic

- School nurse – works with school children and their families

- Special educational needs (SEN) teacher – supports pupils with specialist educational needs

- Social worker – works within the community supporting families and children

- Occupational therapist – helps people who have physical, sensory, or cognitive problems

- Counsellor – helps people overcome their problems with talking therapy, listening to them and encouraging them to make changes to their lives

- CBT therapist – counsellor specializing in cognitive behavioural therapy (CBT), a talking therapy that helps you make positive changes to your thought and behaviour patterns

- Psychiatrist – medical doctor treating people with mental, emotional and behavioural disorders, and prescribing treatment and medication

- Psychologist – therapist using psychotherapy to assess and treat patients with mental, emotional and behavioural disorders

- Mental health nurse – medical professional who cares for and supports people using mental health services

- Dietician – health professional who advises on food and nutrition and may support patients with eating disorders

THE SHARING QUIZ

When I'm feeling sad about something...

a) I prefer to keep it completely to myself – it's too embarrassing to open up to other people

b) I might drop a few hints that I'm not in a good mood, but find it hard to say things directly

c) I will tell a trusted friend or someone in my family so they know I need a bit of extra support – there's no shame in sharing how I'm feeling

When I have a bad day at school...

a) I keep my head down and hope that it all goes away

b) I go home and act moody with my family, but won't tell them why unless they ask

c) I confide in friends and tell my family after school – a problem shared is a problem halved

When bullies are targeting me at school...

a) I don't breathe a word to anyone – won't telling someone just make it worse?

b) it feels too scary to tell anyone except a few close friends at school, but I make them promise not to say anything

c) I realize this won't go away on its own, so I tell someone older that I trust, such as my parents or teacher

If I'm getting overwhelmed with schoolwork, I...

a) plough on, cramming it all in and don't tell anyone that I'm struggling

b) chat and moan to my friends about it

c) ask my parents or teacher for support

If I'm worried about something to do with my health, I...

a) don't want to upset anyone so keep my worries to myself

b) start researching on the internet while I pluck up the courage to tell someone

c) talk to my parents or guardian about seeing my family doctor – there's no point taking chances with my health

Results

Mostly a) You're a private person, who prefers to keep your problems to yourself, but sometimes there are situations that can only be resolved by confiding in others. Sharing your worries is the first step to getting help. Read this chapter to learn how to do that.

Mostly b) You can find it hard opening up to anyone except your closest friends but at times, you need to share your problems with an adult you trust, such as a family member, teacher or your doctor. Reading this chapter will help you know when and how to seek help.

Mostly c) Sharing your feelings comes naturally to you. This is a healthy attitude and means you won't have to cope alone. Recognizing when you need help is a sign of maturity – read the tips in this chapter to know who can offer you that help.

THE ONE THING I'VE NEVER
STOPPED DOING IS ASKING
FOR HELP... THAT WAS
THE HARDEST PART, BUT
I TRULY BELIEVE THAT'S
WHY I'M STRONGER.

SELENA GOMEZ

HOW DO YOU FEEL AND HOW DO YOU WANT TO FEEL?

Write down some words to describe how you're feeling:

Are there some feelings you'd like to change? Write down how you'd like to feel:

ASKING FOR **HELP** ISN'T GIVING UP – IT'S **REFUSING** TO GIVE UP

HELPLINES

If you need to talk about how you're feeling but don't feel able to speak to someone you know, you can call a helpline run by trained people who are ready to listen. Samaritans in the UK and in the USA run helplines, as do other mental health charities worldwide.

The thought of speaking to a stranger on the phone about your problems may seem weird. But sometimes it helps to go over things with someone not involved in your life, who will listen without judging and could help you understand what you're going through.

If you don't want to speak on the phone, some organizations run online chat services allowing you to have a live text conversation with a support worker.

Getting support from a helpline or chat service may help you feel more ready to tell your family and friends how you're feeling, or to seek advice from a professional face to face.

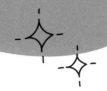

KNOW WHAT TO EXPECT WHEN YOU ASK FOR HELP

It's useful to know how things may pan out after you've asked for help with your mental health. If you've told your parent or guardian that you're worried about your mental health, they may contact your family doctor so you can have an initial appointment to talk about your problem and how it's affecting you.

The doctor may then "refer" you, which means passing you to another health care provider (such as the people mentioned on pages 128–129) who specializes in the area that you need support with.

If you've asked for additional support at school, you may see a professional, such as your school's special educational needs (SEN) teacher or a visiting occupational therapist, within school hours.

KNOW WHAT TO EXPECT FROM YOUR APPOINTMENT

It can be daunting to speak to a professional about your mental health, but addressing your worries is the best way to eventually overcome them – which is what you want, right?

It always helps to be prepared before doing anything new. Of course, every professional is different and your situation is unique to you but there are some general points to know.

You might attend your appointment with your parent or guardian or alone, depending on the situation.

It may help to have some notes prepared so that you know what you want to talk about – and you'll be able to refer to them if you lose your train of thought mid-appointment.

A mental health professional such as a counsellor or therapist (see pages 128–129) will ask questions, such as why you think you've been referred and how you've been coping with your problem up to this point. They may ask how things are at home and school, along with asking you about anything from your past that might be affecting how you're feeling now.

You might be given tasks, such as filling in a form with questions about how you're feeling now and whether you've ever thought about harming yourself. This may seem daunting, especially if it's the first time you've *really* opened up, but it's important to answer honestly so that you get the right support.

BETWEEN APPOINTMENTS

You may be given "homework" to do between your appointments, such as practising mindfulness exercises or jotting a daily record of your feelings.

You may think "but I already get loads of homework from school" and you're not wrong. But it's really important to do *this* work too. You'll get much more out of your treatment if you put the effort in and it will also give your therapist a clearer idea of how you're progressing.

It's also important to turn up to your appointments with time to spare, rather than zooming in at the last minute. By being early, you can take a few moments to focus and gather your thoughts before you begin.

GOING TO HOSPITAL

People get mental health conditions for all kinds of reasons, and in rare cases, a person may need hospital care to ease their mental health issue.

The idea of going to hospital can be frightening, but it's important to remember that hospitals have specialist staff who are there to offer the right treatment and care to help with recovery.

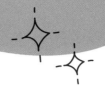

OVERCOMING OBSTACLES

You've already taken one of the hardest steps by asking for help, but working towards recovery can be tough too.

You may wake up some days and feel you're not going anywhere. Well, everyone who's experienced a mental health issue has felt like this at some point but know that things can and will get better for you. Don't give up. You're stronger than you think.

Most importantly, don't be afraid to speak up if you're struggling. Tell your family and friends and also the professionals caring for you, who may be able to adjust your treatment plan if something isn't working.

BUILD A SUPPORT TEAM

Talking about your mental health is really personal and it's understandable if you'd rather keep your problems to yourself.

However, it can actually really help to have a team of "cheerleaders" around you and no, that doesn't mean they should wave pom-poms whenever you attend therapy! But never underestimate the positive power of a quick "how are you doing?" phone call or hug from someone who genuinely cares.

By confiding in two or three friends or relatives about what you're going through, you can share your journey and lighten your mental load a little.

BE YOUR OWN BEST FRIEND

Treat yourself as you'd treat a good friend – with kindness, patience and compassion.

Remind yourself of your successes. Make a note of good days (the tracker chapter in this book will help with this) and try not to dwell too much on down days (look at the self-care chapter for advice on this).

Most important of all, believe in your ability to get through difficult times. It's wonderful to have supportive people around you, but you have to support yourself too.

So be kind to yourself – always.

LIVE MORE, WORRY LESS

HELP YOURSELF

You can have the best people in the world helping you but your recovery can't start unless you have your own best interests at heart.

In other words, you need to know how to help yourself. But how? Well, some of it is down to leading a balanced lifestyle, such as eating well, exercising regularly and getting enough sleep (see pages 76–79).

Recognizing and avoiding unhealthy friendships is also key to aiding your recovery. Think about it for a moment: how can you focus on your own mental health journey if it's constantly being derailed by a "friend" who isn't truly interested in supporting you?

Most important of all when it comes to helping yourself recover is your attitude. When you're feeling low, it's easy to slip into a pattern of thinking that nothing will ever improve. You may think it doesn't matter if you don't turn up to your counselling session for one or two weeks.

But the truth is that it's not enough to let other people do all the hard work. You *have* to take an active role in your treatment plan if it's going to succeed.

That means showing up to every appointment, accepting help and guidance from the professionals and your loved ones and putting in the work.

If you're not having treatment but are focusing on practising more regular self-care, commit to it. Spend a few moments each day thinking about how to take care of yourself and boost your general well-being.

It will be worth it in the end.

Promise.

WORDS TO INSPIRE ME

Think of some words that make you feel happy and excited about life – whether these words describe something you're good at, something you love doing or something that inspires you to look to the future. Write one word inside each cloud and reflect back on these words whenever you need a bit of inspiration.

1

2

3

4

5

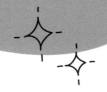

I PROMISE TO...

Write down a promise to yourself that you will keep to improve your mood now and in the future. Revisit this page to remind yourself what you're committing to do – and how it will help you in the future.

_____

_____

_____

_____

_____

_____

_____

_____

_____

_____

_____

CONCLUSION

Congratulations! You've reached the end of this book. Hopefully you now understand more about the changes going on in your body and brain along with some of your mood triggers. You should also now be aware of the most commonly experienced mental health issues in people your age.

Take a look back at chapter four and read through your completed tracker pages. Are there any noticeable patterns? Any simple changes that you could make to your lifestyle – do you need more sleep or to improve your diet? Never forget the importance of self-care.

Most importantly, you should now feel able to seek support when you need it. Keep in mind that everyone goes through challenges in life and that asking for help is a sign of true strength.

Refer back to the tips on these pages whenever you feel that you need a mood boost or some pointers. By understanding yourself and your feelings, you'll have the power and emotional knowledge to live your best life – now and always.

Good luck.

YOU DON'T NEED TO JUSTIFY
YOUR MENTAL HEALTH
TO ANYONE. PRIORITIZE
YOURSELF WHEN NEEDED,
TAKE TIME TO REST.
SURROUND YOURSELF
WITH GOOD PEOPLE... AND
TOMORROW COULD BE
SUCH A BEAUTIFUL DAY.

LILI REINHART

FINDING FURTHER SUPPORT

Looking for more information, guidance or help? Here are some useful organizations to know about.

- **Ditch the Label** – tackles young people's mental-health issues globally. **www.ditchthelabel.org/**

- **NHS** – offers an online directory of UK health services, which is handy if you want to speak to a medical professional such as a doctor in your local area but aren't sure where to find them. **www.nhs.uk/Service-Search**

- **Children and young people's mental health services (CYPMHS)** – the UK-based NHS services that assess and treat young people with emotional, behavioural or mental health difficulties along with neurodivergent conditions. You may also see the term **children and adolescent mental health services (CAMHS)** used, depending on provision in your area. **www.nhs.uk/mental-health/children-and-young-adults**

- **World Health Organization** – a global agency dedicated to helping people live healthy lives. Guided by science, they offer news articles and advice on all health matters including mental health for young people. **www.who.int**

- **Young Minds** – a charity that provides mental health information and advice to young people and parents and carers. **www.youngminds.org.uk/**

- **Mental Health Foundation** – offers advice on mental health problems as well as doing research into mental health and lobbying lawmakers. **www.mentalhealth.org.uk/**

- **Mind** – a charity that offers guidance on getting help for mental health problems. Email **info@mind.org.uk** or call the Mind infoline on 0300 123 3393 (UK landline calls are charged at local rates, and charges from mobile phones vary). **www.mind.org.uk/**

- **Samaritans** – a charity that offers emotional support in confidence 24/7. In the UK, email **jo@samaritans.org.uk** or call for free on 116 123. **www.samaritans.org/** – other suicide-prevention charities are available worldwide.

- **Shout** – can help with urgent issues such as suicidal thoughts, self-harm, bullying or abuse. In the UK, text Shout to 85258 and get free 24/7 mental health text support. **www.giveusashout.org/**

- **Beat** – an eating disorder charity that offers a free helpline and one-on-one web chat service. You don't need a formal eating disorder diagnosis to use their services. **www.beateatingdisorders.org.uk/**

- **National Bullying Helpline** – supports young people who are being bullied and their families. www.nationalbullyinghelpline.co.uk/

- **National Autistic Society** – for parents of autistic children, young autistic people and autistic adults, this charity offers a services directory so you can find support in your area. www.autism.org.uk

- **ADHD Foundation Neurodiversity Charity** – offers support for people living with ADHD, autism, dyslexia, dyspraxia, dyscalculia and Tourette syndrome. www.adhdfoundation.org.uk/

- **Stonewall** – the largest LGBTQ+ rights organization in Europe, offering support and advice to young people and their families. www.stonewall.org.uk/

A NOTE FROM THE PEER REVIEWER

Louise's book is an engaging read. I liked her supportive interactive style that remained adult in its approach. She has a good understanding of the pressures on young people today and offers sound advice for mental and physical health and well-being.

Mayvrill Freeston-Roberts, BACP Accredited and Registered Counsellor and Psychotherapist

NOTES

Have you enjoyed this book?
If so, why not write a review on your favourite website?

If you're interested in finding out more about our books,
find us on Facebook at **Summersdale Publishers**, on
Twitter at **@Summersdale** and on Instagram
at **@summersdalebooks** and get in touch.
We'd love to hear from you!

Thanks very much for buying this Summersdale book.

www.summersdale.com

Image credits